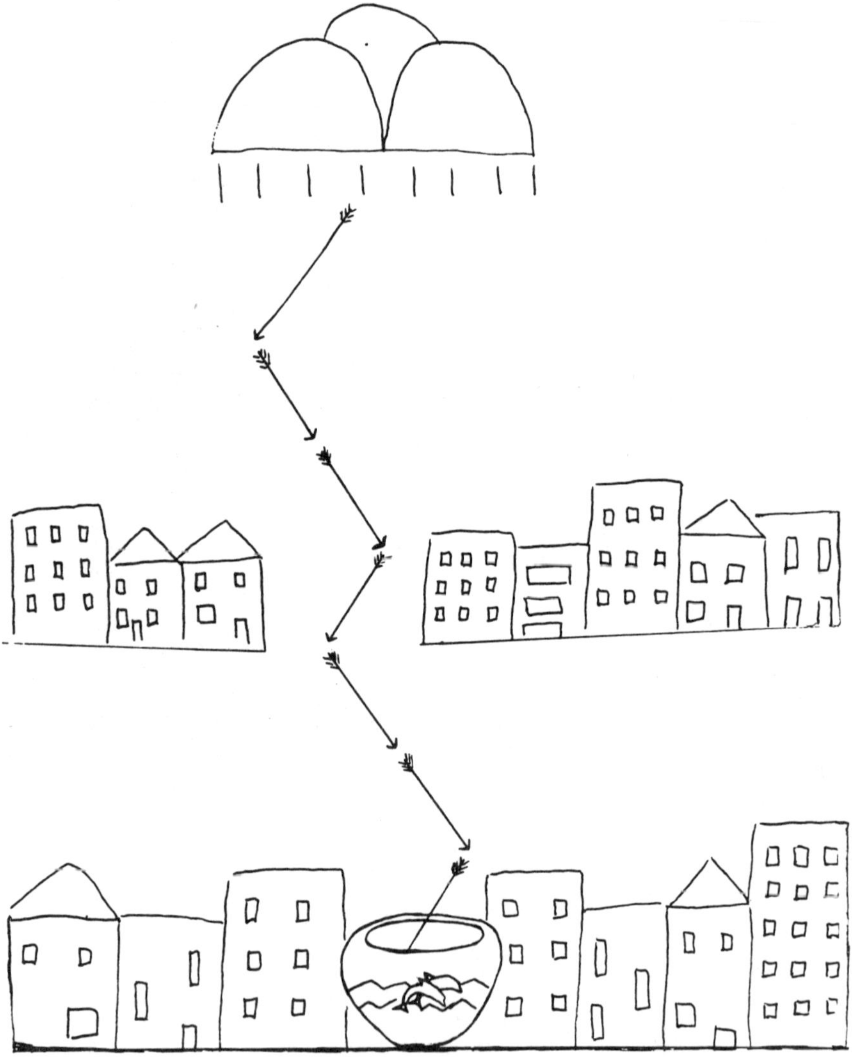

THE WAY OF THE

RAINBOW WARRIORESS

A Handbook of Practical Wisdom

El Rancho Press
P.O. Box 41725
Santa Barbara, CA 93140-1725

The Way of the Rainbow Warrioress:
A Handbook of Practical Wisdom

Cover design and illustrations by Janice Tucker

Printed in the United States of America.

ACKNOWLEDGEMENTS

I extend my thanks and gratitude to

Lynn Andrews for her personal guidance as well as for the inspiration within her books

James Barnett, formerly Swami Buddhananda, for his hospitality and wisdom, for some perspective on the difference between power and spirituality, and for pointing out the magic within the ordinary

A medicine teacher who prefers not to be named for the teachings in his books, workshops and a few personal encounters before he traveled paths that I would not care to follow

The authors whose words I have quoted in this book

The teachers who guided my studies in Jungian psychology

My sisters and brothers of the Sun Tribe for their sharing within ceremony and friendship

Snow Deer for her friendship, encouragement, and for just quietly living her medicine

Tom Phillips for the use of his computer

My horses, my cat, and my dog for medicine teachings from the animal world and for keeping me on a path with a heart

My inner teachers.

I dedicate this book
to my mother and father
in appreciation for
their confidence, support and T.L.C.

CONTENTS

INTRODUCTION

During her readings and lectures, one of the questions most commonly asked of Lynn Andrews, author of a series of books on Native American female shamanism, goes something like this:

> "Lynn, I have two children, a husband and a full time job. How can I apply your experience and the teaching in your books to my own life? There is no way I can leave the city to study with a medicine woman in Canada, even if she would deign to teach me."

After I heard that question a few times, I realized that I could begin to answer it.

Shortly after Lynn Andrews published her first book, *Medicine Woman*, I became her student and continued to meet with her in the following years whenever that far-ranging, ground-covering woman would sit down long enough in the circle of her wolf tail. In her first four books, *Medicine Woman, Flight of the Seventh Moon, Jaguar Woman, and Star Woman,* she describes with the flare of an expert story teller her apprenticeship with Native American women in Canada and the Yucatan. I, however, met with Lynn in restaurants and in her modest Beverly Hills home, never in a forest, cave, cabin, or jungle. Much primal wisdom can be assimilated and put into practice by modern urban women and men.

This book is an interweaving of narrative and practical applications (how-to's) based on my experience under the guidance not only of Lynn Andrews and other medicine teachers, but also that of my own inner teachers. These applications include instructions for making and working with a medicine wheel; making masks and other symbolic images; discovering the warrioress and warrior within you; gaining insights into such concepts as the sacred spiral, tonal, power, sacred words, and ceremony; and communicating with dream animals and other inner teachers.

This book is a beginning place, only a first guidepost on a longer journey far beyond its ending. Good medicine to you as you take the first step along this way. Here is a traveling song, taught to me by one of my inner teachers, for you to sing as you go:

Sun shining in joy, Sun of love
Sun of soul, Sun of beauty, glorious knowing
Sun, Sun, enveloping brightness
Sun, Sun, lifting the pattern
Sun of loving, pattern for knowing
Sun of the universe and of the mind
Sun of love, Sun forever, Sun together, wholeness
Sun above, Sun below
Sun enter my soul.

BEFORE YOU IS THE UNIVERSE. REMEMBER THAT ALL THINGS ARE SACRED.

- Twin Dreamers
in *Star Woman*

CHAPTER ONE

SACRED ANIMALS

Little Miss Muffet
sat on a tuffet
eating her curds and whey.
Along came a spider
and sat down beside her...

A huge, hairy black spider approached me, larger than myself. My terror woke me. After reassuring myself in the familiarity of my bedroom, I returned to the dream.

"Spider Woman," I said to her, "You feel much too close for comfort, and you frighten me, but seem to be a friend. What do you want?"

"Friendship in return," she replied. "Your life is being woven. You may as well participate."

Then she went on to explain to me other things that I needed to know.

Applying the wisdom of Native American spiritual traditions and shamanic lore, as well as the wisdom of other spiritual traditions, means making our lives sacred once again, or rather, recognizing the sacredness of all that is. Life is no longer mundane, an accumulation of meaningless moments. Instead, you are special and worthy of love. All life, *the web of life*, on this planet is part of a divine dance, a weaving, a dance cape; each act is part of this larger movement in which you are *consciously participating* in your own unique way.

Much of what Lynn Andrews learned from her Native American teachers and what she, in turn, teaches to others involves recreating and living in sacred space and sacred time, knowing the larger circle of ourselves and giving form to our knowledge.

It is a special task of our time to create a bridge between ancient (and inner) wisdom and modern industrial urbanized cultures, assimilating and balancing both, creating a new way that is neither one nor the other for the sake of healing ourselves and this planet. To create such a bridge is the way of the rainbow warrioress.

As Spider Woman told me, "You cannot tarry too long. Change must come."

"And how do I give way to change?" I asked.

"Collect your thoughts." she replied. "Do not scatter them like straw in the wind.... There is much to learn."

...And there are many teachers, not the least of who are the sacred animal comrades who "people" our lives.

Since most of us will not have such dramatic adventures and medicine teachers as Lynn Andrews had, I want to tell you a story. I want to do this partly to introduce myself and my companions to you and partly to show how an ordinary person can find magic and wondrous mirroring in the most ordinary events.

Although the events in the following story took place several years before I became interested in Native American lore, it illustrates concepts which were confirmed and amplified in later learning, such as

1. Taking one's own authority (after first making the mistake of giving one's power away.)

2. Relating to dreams and whatever creatures and events occur therein.

3. Acknowledging the animals in one's life as relatives and teachers.

4. Connecting to, validating, and strengthening the feminine principle in oneself.

5. Learning about self and values through a decision making process.

6. Symbolic magical ritual.

7. Active receptivity.

8. *Perseverance,* a required character trait in a warrioress. At its roots perseverance means *truth to self.*

PERSEVERANCE OF A MARE

My mare sings through me
Butt against back
Three beats to a measure!

"When are you going to sell your horses?" asked the psychologist whom I was seeing in those days, dropping the question casually.

"Sell my horses! I would never do that!"

But the man had authority in my psyche. I began to think, "Maybe that is what would be best for me, the only way to get out of this rut of non-achievement that I am in. I could go back to school to acquire a degree in a worthwhile profession so that I could support myself more effectively. The horses cost so much. They take so much time."

His suggestion grew like yellow star thistles in my mind. No matter that the horses were the center of my life. No matter that I loved them. What an impractical, childish self-indulgence. No matter that caring for them had kept me grounded and functioning in the depression that had followed the suicide of a dear friend.

He planted the seed; but I watered it, tended it, grew it, and sold my horses six months later. My gelding would live only a mile away where I could visit him occasionally, but my mare went to another city to become a teenage girl's show jumper.

I returned to school to achieve my third master's degree. Maybe this one--in psychology--would net me some money, status and power in the world as well as some personal satisfaction from helping others. Unable, thus far, to compete successfully in a limited job market with my other two degrees, I seemed always to be scraping the bottom of the barrel for any work I could find. How I longed for the day when I could command fifty instead of five dollars per hour.

But I missed my horses! Their loss was a heart wound. Becoming a successful woman of the world was exacting too great a price. During my course of study with an understanding supervisor, however, I became more aware of the feeling, receptive, and intuitive sides of myself, aspects which I often experienced but had never *valued*. These perspectives began to balance the patriarchally favored goal and achievement oriented values and my consequent sense of failure. I quit working with the psychologist who could not understand why I grieved for my horses.

As I neared the end of my study program, I learned that my mare was for sale. The girl had become interested in boys. Isharra (whose name is a variant of Ishtar, the Sumerian goddess) stood in her stall day after day, cast aside and neglected as her namesake had been by the advent of patriarchy. The girl's mother called me to ask if I were interested in buying her back. It seemed a remarkable synchronicity--a chance to *redeem* her, buy her back, just as I finished the course of study that her sale had financed. Ready to pay the price--twice the amount for which I had sold her--I excitedly told them to bring her right home.

Suddenly I felt some resistance, became confused and decided to wait a bit to try to figure out what was stopping me. Apparently, even though I had jettisoned that psychologist, I myself possessed a good measure of the logic and sensibility that I associated with him.

I said to myself, "It would be silly to buy my mare back just because it would make me feel good. Besides, it's a raw deal. She costs too much. I can't afford her."

To help resolve my indecision I consulted the *I Ching*, an ancient Chinese book of oracular wisdom, and drew the hexagram "Youthful Folly". I certainly did feel as if I were about to leap blindly into an abyss in this transaction, as the *I Ching* described, for it would empty my bank account; yet the change lines referred me to the hexagram "*K'un*, the Receptive", which read as follows:

> The RECEPTIVE brings about sublime success,
> Furthering through the perseverance of a mare...[!][1]

Symbolizing the *receptive* aspect of the feminine principle, this mare is described as roaming unbounded over the earth, gentle, yielding, persevering and strong, her strength a necessary support for *creative* action.

This remarkable coincidence, so typical of the *I Ching*, spoke to the wisdom of my heart and harmonized with my fledgling efforts to understand and to live the principle of receptivity. Receptivity is, paradoxically, active. It is a consciously chosen attitude that involves alertness, awareness and readiness to act or create. I was not just determining to buy a horse; I was forging a philosophy and path of life that would reflect feminine balance into the world. Thus encouraged, I prepared to leap into the abyss, trusting in life. At least I could consciously choose my own folly.

Then head spoke to heart saying, "Just deal with it on a symbolic level, little fool. That way won't cost money."

For over a month I stalled in excruciating indecision until one night, in a dream, a little skunk began to follow me. I tried to escape, but he was persistent and tangled himself up in my legs. When I woke up I realized he had just been trying to get my attention. Having learned during my psychological studies that, just as in fairy tales, helper animals sometimes come to us in dreams to advise and guide us, I decided to converse with the skunk, a dialog within the imagination.

"Well, little skunk, what is it?"

"Listen to your heart and soul," he replied. "Buy your mare."

"Why should I buy her? She costs too much."

"Cost cannot be measured in money," he said.

"Is it really my mare you came to see me about?"

"Yes, she is more important than you recognize."

"Why, Skunk, why?"

"She lightens your heart."

"Yes, but there are other considerations. What about practicality, finances?"

"You'll manage. Have faith. That's what it's all about."

"Why are you so friendly, Skunk?"

"Ah! I thought you would never ask. Jan, do not forget your path. Waiting, receptive. Humor. Remember me. Hold me in your heart when you talk with others. When you want to say something, consult me; keep me by your side. Aggression and assertiveness are not necessary, as I can show you. You do not need to teach." (referring, I think, to my tendency to be aggressively pedantic)

"But, little fellow, I have no stink!"

"You have been known to raise one, now and then. Just go your way. The path will clear for you as it does for me.

"But I don't always know what my path is," I argued disconsolately.

"You have been learning all along. And
I'll let you know when you have gone astray--so watch out!"

I sulked. "I wish the signals could be so concrete!" Then I cheered up a bit and said to him, "I like talking to you. I look in your eyes and what do I find there? Old wisdom. I keep seeing those dead skunks on the road though."

"A skunk is not safe from inhuman machines," he replied.

"Skunks also carry madness." I said.

"Yes, there is darkness. See the light now, Jan, the joy of relationship with me, that delight of recognition and conspiracy. Let's create a little comedy as we ramble through the woods, I first, you following.

We will get where you want to go,
The beginning and end of the rainbow."

That conversation solved my dilemma. I no longer had any doubt about which course to take. I called Isharra's owners to say I would buy her.

"We just sold her this morning," they said and refused to tell me the name and address of the new owners.

I hung up the phone and cried.

After a few despondent weeks, having decided I wanted a horse in my life again, feeling almost compulsive about it, I began a search for the right horse. But I found none. Oh, there was a sweet appaloosa with a coat like mithril; but he cost as much as my mare, and he was still untrained. In addition, he bit me. There was a recently gelded young Morgan for sale. He had beauty and charisma, but he was just too macho.

During this time, unable to accomplish my task of obtaining the right horse by direct action, I went for a contemplative walk on a mountain jeep trail. On a whim, I sat down right in the middle of the dirt road and drew a circle in the soil with a horse in the center--just as ancient hunters might have done to ensure a successful hunt.

Two weeks later I received a phone call from Isharra's new owners: "Our daughter can't handle her. Isharra keeps bucking her off." (Isharra had never behaved like that!) "Would you like to buy her? We understand you were interested before we purchased her."

I paid her price without even trying to bargain and brought her home. Now my life was in harmony--a ravaged but replaceable bank account, my mare in her corral and some new insight into the meaning of active receptivity.

Just as I had conducted a conversation with the dream skunk, I spoke now with my beautiful mare:

"What does the horse mean? Isharra, speak!"

"I am your guide into the wilderness. With me you fly. With me you see."

"Together we go, sister, friend."

"My sister, my friend, let us not again be parted."

"You have my pledge."

I have kept my pledge to Isharra. Whenever I need to recover balance and strength in the female side of myself, I visit her in her pasture at night, where I sit on the ground and sing or play a drum softly to her while she stands over me as over a foal, softly nuzzling my hair. And although I know now that many a horse has carried a shamaness on her journeys into the wilderness of another reality, it is enough that my spirit soars when I watch her running, rearing, tossing her head with the joy of life in her; and I see that the medicine is in our everyday interactions.

CHAPTER TWO

SACRED SPACE

CIRCLES

Long ago in a dream , before I had ever heard of medicine wheels, I sat on a chair in a room in the middle of a zoo. A snake circled my chair several times. Later, outside, I saw a red ring containing a giant, throbbing, undulating, coiled creature.

After I woke up I spoke with this being.

Who are you, round thing?
    A ring.
I know, but who are you?
    A ring of life.
What do you mean?
    Life awaits every one.
I don't understand.
    In the ring is all knowing.
What do you want me to know?
    Yourself and all the land.
That's nonsense to me. Give me words I understand.
    Center yourself, girl! Let the ring surround you!
What does the ring mean?
    Life and love.
Life and love, Mother?
    Life all nourishing, love in depth.

* *

The Jungian analyst June Singer noted that a suffering human being who comes into analysis has "lost the sense of primordial wholeness that represents the paradise of innocence. He is troubled, feels separated from the world or from the mystery which he intuitively knows as his real self. His equilibrium is shaken. He needs to be made whole again." [2]

One of the symbols, common to most cultures and religious traditions, of this balance, harmony and all-encompassing wholeness is the circle. *Mandala*, the Sanskrit word for circle, has become nearly a household word in recent decades, inspired by an increase of interest in Eastern philosophical and spiritual traditions. The rose window in Christian cathedrals is an example of a mandala, as is the historical site of Stonehenge, many sand paintings of the Hopi and Navajo, the design of the original city of Jerusalem and of Washington, D.C., and the dolphin fountain in Santa Barbara, California.

In Native American tradition, this circle is known as a medicine wheel. It is a circle of symbols and concepts used to teach and to express understanding of balance and harmony within the universe and within each individual human being. A circle also forms the sacred space in which most ceremonies take place.

The medicine wheel is complex and many layered, the non-cardinal directions also defined. The following diagrams show some of the concepts associated with the four primary directions of the medicine wheel--North, South, East and West. It is important to realize, however, that different tribes and cultures associate various concepts with different parts of the circle. The essential characteristics remain balance and wholeness.

MEDICINE WHEEL

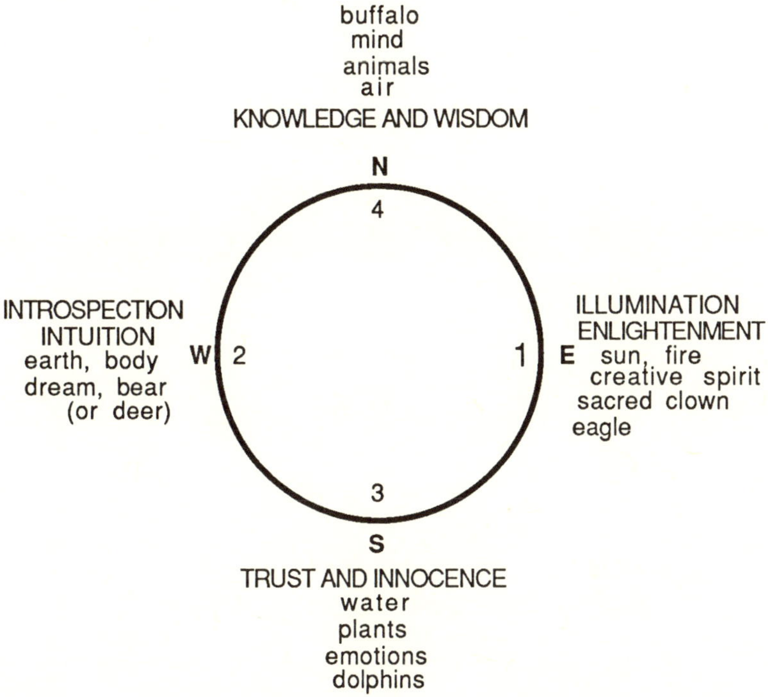

Note: The numbers are part of the **twenty count,** a sacred numerology.

WOMAN'S SHIELD

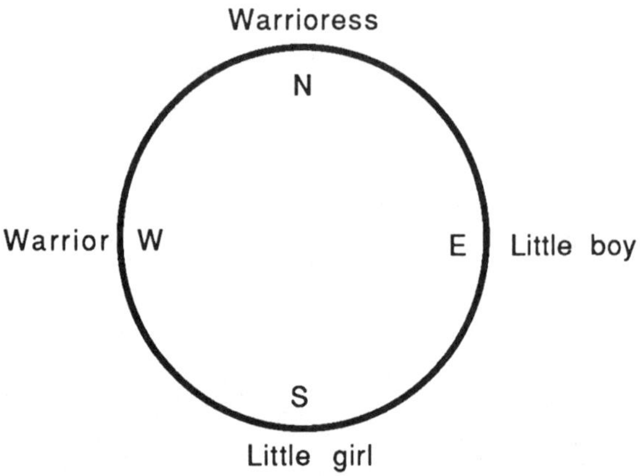

MAN'S SHIELD

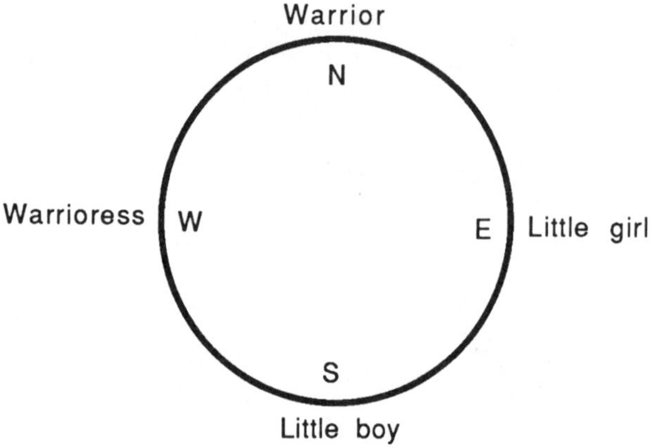

In her book *Flight of the Seventh Moon*, Lynn Andrews experiences the process of working in each of the four directions, moving clockwise around the wheel. It is a process of becoming acquainted with herself. For each direction she makes a shield which symbolically represents her understanding. She describes the fruition of this process in a final ceremony:

> I began to pray. I heard the coyotes howling again, or perhaps it was the howling wind in the distance. The rock beneath the blanket began to feel cold. Carefully, I unwrapped my four shields and placed them in their four directions around me... The shields stood for the concept of who I am in my completeness. Together they were the ultimate medicine wheel, the map from my outer to my inner being. To conceive of them was to conceive of the mystery of my oneness...They were my very personification. The fifth shield was me, the void, the grandmother, the self. I sat in front of my south shield and sang her song of trust and innocence. I repeated this in front of each shield, prayed and sang in front of the west for good medicine dreams and the rebirth of my spirit. I prayed and sang to the north for understanding and wisdom to fulfill my dreams and visions. Then to the heyoka east shield, I asked and sang for illumination. I made offerings of tobacco to each shield and then I smoked the pipe again in the center, the place of the Rainbow Chiefs, the seat of the invisible shield where all knowledge and spirit come together to secure form and direction. I stretched my hands to the sky. Agnes had taught me to open myself at this point in the ceremony and to hold an image of my

> shields as part of a shattered mirror fitted
> at once together to make a whole.[3]

One day, you too can perform this ceremony, for you have the greatest, wisest, most powerful medicine teacher of all. *Life*, our experience of life, is the medicine woman who teaches most of us the understanding of the four directions and places us, if we have learned our lessons, in the center of our circle.

APPLICATIONS

Let the ring surround you! A medicine wheel can be created in your room, in your back yard, in a mountain meadow, or by the intentional direction of your glance. The best introduction to the medicine wheel that I know of is in the beginning of the book *Seven Arrows* by Hyemeyohsts Storm.

The circumference and points on a medicine wheel can be represented with pebbles, rocks, flowers, corn meal, tobacco, sand painting, and even aesthetic landscaping. Here are just a few suggestions for ways you can work with this special circle. *Doing* these things, rather than just reading about them is a way to begin taking personal power.

1. Acknowledge and pray to the Four Directions, Sun, and Earth each morning.

2. Sit in each of the four directions of your circle. See what each feels like, keeping symbols and images of associated concepts in your mind. Note where you feel most at home.

For example, as you sit in the South of your circle, become a tree, your roots deep in the earth, your branches open to the wind and sun. Think of dolphins, too, creatures of trust and innocence playing in the sea. Remember that the South is the place of the girl child within you, the little girl who you once were. Allow that child to *be*. Young girls once were taught to love their bodies, their cycles, their thoughts, their feelings, their femaleness. You may need to begin your own medicine journey by re-turning temporarily to the girl child within you to re-nurture and re-value her. She is the seed from which the adult woman grows.

In the North, on the other hand, you will need to hold the power, wisdom and knowledge of the warrioress within you. North is the place of the give-away of that knowledge and wisdom to your children and to the world-at-large, food for the people like the great buffalo. In the North lives also White Buffalo Woman (also known as Wisdom Woman, White Clay Woman, White Tara, Sophia, and other names), who brought the medicine pipe to the People so they could send their voices to the Great Spirit.

3. Sit in the *center* of the medicine wheel. Here you will be mediating and balancing all parts of the circle. You must not identify with any of them. Speak to your little girl in the South, to your warrior in the West, to your warrioress in the North, to your little boy in the East. These beings are within you, a part of your whole circle. If you are able, listen to their voices too. (In chapter 5 you will learn how to become acquainted with your warrioress and your warrior.) Men will orient themselves somewhat differently, as pointed out in the two shield diagrams.

4. Draw a circle on a piece of paper. Divide it into four pie slices for each direction. Write your goals for the next five years in the appropriate quarter. Will your life be in balance?

For example, your goals in the *South* might have to do with relating to the children in your life, as well as to the child within yourself. In some way you might want to make the plant world a part of your life--anything from gardening to ecological activism, depending on your own nature. With the image and symbol of water in mind, perhaps one of your goals will be to allow the life force to flow more freely within yourself and all aspects of your life.

In the *West* your goals might include relating to your dreams (What is your dream of life?);

relating to inner and outer men; allowing time in your life for introspection; caring for your body through attitude, proper food and exercise; and caring for the mother Earth.

In the *North* sector define your career goals along with the material things you want to acquire: a certain level of income, a particular kind of house, etc. Here you might also set goals concerning sisterhood and your relationships with other women as well as with your inner warrioress. Perhaps you will have goals in connection with the animal teachers that share this time and space on earth with you. Consider also what kind of knowledge and wisdom you really want to achieve and, in turn, give away to others.

In the *East* your goals might include your spiritual aspirations and your creativity--whatever form they may take. What do you want to bring to birth in the world? What do you want to make, to create? Getting in touch with the little boy in yourself, what kinds of adventures do you want to engage in? Perhaps a spiritual quest or journey or a vision quest belongs in this sector of your goal wheel.

5. Now draw the circle again, this time illustrating your goals with pictures and symbols. You have just made a shield!

DO IT! Draw the circle on this page. Divide it into four sectors. Define your goals.

Draw the circle again on this page, this time using illustrations in the four sectors instead of words.

ALTARS

Like the medicine wheel, an altar also becomes sacred space for tapping inner wisdom and life energy through ceremony, meditation, song and prayer. A corner, a table, or a whole room can be transformed into an altar. Some altars are extremely complex in both symbol and structure, including both the dark and the light. In *Jaguar Woman* such an altar is called "the face of the earth." If you are a beginner in these ways, keep it simple for now. The more conscious you become, so also might your altar become more complex to reflect that consciousness. (Sand tray therapy is a modern psychotherapeutic version of the working altar.) Following are a few suggestions for creating your own altar.

To strengthen, honor, know and love the female principle within you and to mirror your own divine nature, place a Goddess image on your altar. (If a woman and her altar have a male *bias*, her altar will be dead.) Men, too, who understand that balance is needed within themselves and within the world, are placing the Goddess on their altars. She might be Artemis, Kwan Yin, Tara, the Virgin Mary, the black Madonna, or an unknown Indian woman with a bowl in her lap. Bring her flowers. Make your altar a place of beauty, remembering, however, that what it represents is not separate from you or outside yourself, but a reflection of you. Remember also that ultimately, ideally, your altar should represent wholeness, including female and male balance.

You may also want to place objects on your altar that have meaning for you--medicine objects such as fetishes, feathers, medicine bundles, totem symbols. Take your own authority in these matters. Allow the altar to reflect yourself. Whenever you place something on your altar, accompany it with an offering. *Words are an offering.*

CHAPTER THREE

SPIRIT WORDS

* *

Shaman words return your spirit
Lost spirit of the great earth round
I return to the women of mystery
The spirit words that have been lost.

-Lynn Andrews
Flight of the Seventh Moon

* *

* *

For she was the maker of the song she sang.
The ever-hooded, tragic-gestured sea
Was merely a place by which she walked to sing.
Whose spirit is this? we said, because we knew
It was the spirit that we sought and knew
That we should ask this often as she sang.

-Wallace Stevens
from "Ideas of Order
at Key West"

* *

Language is sacred in Native American healing and spiritual traditions. Words have power. Repetition of words generates even more power. Stories are told and chants are sung within ceremony that transport the participants into the sacred time and space of the tribal mythology and healing imagery.

Maria Sabina, a Mazatec shamaness of Mexico relates:

> If music sounds I dance as a partner with the Principal Ones; and I also see that words fall, they come from up above, as if they were little luminous objects falling from the sky. The language falls on the sacred table, falls on my body. Then with my hands I catch word after word...and I sing...[4]

such words as

> I am a woman who shouts, says
> I am a woman who whistles, says
> I am a woman who thunders, says
> I am a woman who plays music, says
> I am a spirit woman, says[5]

From the point of view of another spiritual tradition, Swami Muktananda (of India) wrote of the sacred nature of language as one with Shakti, the feminine principle, divine mother of the universe, the supreme creative power:

> She is Brahman in the form of sound, the sound vibration of the Absolute, which manifested the universe. In mantras, She is of the form of...the letters, and in words She is the form of knowledge...It is She who

brings sound, language and alphabet into existence. So She is alive in all the letters of the alphabet, from beginning to end.[6]

Zoila, a medicine teacher in *Jaguar Woman*, posed the question: "Why do shamans go around chanting all the time and making weird noises?" Then she explained that every form has a sound. "If you want to seduce a spirit and make it yours, one of the things you do is sing to it. Words, sounds, tone, they are all part of what holds our reality together. Never is there a life form without sound."[7]

* * * * * * * * * * * * * *

One day, after speaking with a medicine teacher from whom I had sought knowledge, I went to a clearing in a woods to meditate on our conversation and to perform ceremony related to the four directions of the medicine wheel. Suddenly there occurred a click and an unusual sensation in my right ear.

Then I became aware of the tree behind me making sounds that I had not heard before and which could not be explained by the light breeze blowing. It seemed to me that the tree was singing! I tried to imitate its sounds as well as I could with my human voice. In long drawn-out syllables, changing and circling in pitch, I sang:

Aaaaaa, Eeeeee, Iiiiii, Oooooo
Aaaaaa, Eeeeee, Iiiiii, Oooooo
A I O
A I O

How amazingly pleasurable it was to sing those simple vowel sounds. It became a chant that I sang over and over in harmony with the tree. The tree sang on when I became quiet, then subsided. I thanked it for this beautiful blessing, for teaching me this song, and offered it tobacco.

Now I think I understand when I am told of the "tree alphabet" and that humans learned the alphabet from trees.

* * * * * * * * * * * * * *

Another time, many years ago, I opened a refrigerator and out of the freezer slid a completely skinned, dead and frozen man. My terror as he lay on the floor in front of me, raw meat with his mouth widely agape, woke me from the dream.

In the safety of daylight I recalled the vision to my mind. It had occurred to me that a flayed man who had died with his mouth wide open must have something he wanted to say; so, feeling a mixture of compassion and revulsion, I asked him to speak. As I recorded his words, he said:

"In the beginning when the Word was and only the Word, the Word created God, who then created the world. The Word was love in the world, love extended through the Word. Love is the creator, the binding force, that which brings nature into being more than mere energy. The Word gathers the earth, shaping it, gathers the pieces, all the scattered things. Word, Word, the truth, the beginning, gathering like a kind father all creation to his heart. Open your own mouths in praise of the Word. Let the praise fly like doves from your mouth.

"In the depths, in the caves, back, back in time, deep down, the Word appeared as wonder among the beasts called men. Speech began, a wonder, the treasure of the race. How they danced and wondered speechless around the Word, for the Word was still outside them. The Word was like a solid rock, numinous before them. Soon these beasts became conscious of the sounds the birds and other beasts around them made. They likened these sounds to the singing of their own rock and began imitating the rock, which was the Word. They became conscious of their own sounds and began to play and revel in them, only a game at first, a sacred game because it was still in honor of the rock. Gradually, as these early humans absorbed the lore of the rock, internalized it, the Word, the rock, lost its numinosity. Men took it for their own and forgot the beginning, forgot the wonder of the Word. The Word became profane, the tool of everyday life, a tool to be used and tossed uncared for, like a dull knife, into the corner.

"Yet speech contains its own original wonder and the poets of today have begun to gather in the scattered word, bringing the mundane, profane words back into their arms, close to the heart, each word a treasured artifact on the dump of human history.

"As the Word was once loving father to the man, so man is becoming, must become, loving father to the Word. The Word has taken man far and now man must honor the Word, understand the Word, trace the artifacts on the dump back to the beginnings, know the whole story, now at the end."

This flayed man spoke of an ending. I did not ask him what he meant. I thought perhaps he meant the end of an age, a patriarchal age; certainly his speech is in strictly masculine terms. Many years later a time known as the *Harmonic Convergence* has marked a cosmic movement into a new cycle, a new age. A medicine teacher to whom I spoke about this speech said that it was prophecy, not meant just for me. This voice, in praise of the Word, is to flow outward into the future, into the coming Changing Times. Whether perceived as masculine or feminine Logos, the Word is a treasure that must be recognized and saved from complete desacralization. Origins must be remembered. Without sound there is no form. Men must indeed become fathers to the Word; and women must become its mothers, giving form to love through words.

Love, love, enduring brightness
Love is the only and all.
In the tall arch of understanding
Love is the end and the beginning.

-an inner teacher

APPLICATIONS

As an inner teacher once told me,

Sing from your heart
Sing from your soul
You will be whole.

1. Sing whatever sounds, syllables, words that come to you as you observe a flower, a tree, your cat, your dog, your children or anything else in your surroundings. Play and revel in the sounds and in the simple joy of singing. Talent is not required.

   However, a word to the wise: I once lay on the beach in my bikini soaking up the sun, a straw hat over my face. The sound of the waves, the warmth and texture of the sand under my fingers, the heat of the sun, the radiant earth energy around me surged into song, and I began warbling away under my hat. After a time I peeked out and noticed a few people walking warily around me, looking at me rather in askance. So, if you are shy and easily embarrassed, you may want to begin your vocal adventuring in a place more private than the kiva in the crown of your hat.

2. Pick up a drum. Begin beating whatever rhythms suit you. Add sounds, syllables, words if you wish. Express your feelings. Let the song rise from within. It is a kind of meditation.

3. Say or sing a *mantra* that feels right to you. A *mantra*, although it is a term that derives from India, often means a God or Goddess name in any

spiritual tradition. Sacred mantras are sounds that are related to higher beings who can be called into assistance, into your presence. Each mantra creates a mandala that "goes out" and attracts one of these beings. Some Native Americans are given sacred songs in visions or by a teacher that will allow a particular spirit to manifest.

4. Discover the origins of the words you use. At the same time, you will be witnessing your own origins. One way to embark on this adventure is to look up the roots of words in the dictionary, especially words that resonate for you and occur frequently in your vocabulary. The American Heritage Dictionary (2nd ed.), with its list of Indo-European roots, is a good resource.

   For example, look up the words "trust" and "innocence", which define the attitude associated with South on the medicine wheel. *Innocence*, at its roots, means *not to harm.* *Trust* derives from the same root word as *tree.* Plants are also located in the South on this version of the wheel, so that *trust* takes on the meaning of standing rooted in the mother earth like a tree and, from that sturdy position, biding life, sustained from above and below. South is also the place of the child within you. *Trust* and *innocence* are that childlike attitude, "that original state in which we are in rapport with nature and its transpersonal energies which guide and support."[8]

5. Replace negative verbal "self-talk" with positive affirmations spoken aloud or silently.

6. Write poems, songs, stories, if you are so inclined. To do so in a medicine way is a form of worship, of love-making, not just a path to a talk show.

7. Pray

8. Here are two simple chants that you might enjoy singing:

    Na Nin De He
    He Yo Ya Ne
    I am using my heart.

    Hi-na-ne-he, Ki, Ne, Na, We, Man-i-do
    I am swinging the spirit like a child.

CHAPTER FOUR

MASKS, FETISHES AND OTHER IMAGES

Once, out of the shimmering distance, an old woman approached me, chanting and dancing. Dressed in a baggy brown dress, she looked like an old brown potato. When she arrived in front of me, her appearance changed into that of a woman in modern dress, and her song changed, too, from a chant of the earth to an earthy cabaret song. When I awoke I spoke with her.

Old dancing woman, who are you?
    I dance close to earth, to wholeness. I dance the body and the soul.
What were you singing?
    A song of life.
What were you dancing?
    A dance of love.
What are life and love?
    Knowing and understanding.
Is there any way but words?
    Experience.

There was more to the conversation, but that is enough. Her dance was within me, her dance and her song. They were a treasure, and I thanked her.

* * * * * * * * * * * * * *

BODY MIND AND DREAM BODY

One afternoon I met with Lynn Andrews at a local restaurant. I had had an irritating cough for some time and constantly felt the need to clear my throat. While I ate, some food became stuck in my throat, until I coughed the blockage up. Right then and there, Lynn halted all other conversation and sent me on a journey to my throat.

I didn't give logical, mental mind a chance to tell me that it was impossible for me to take a stroll in my own throat. Sitting there at the restaurant table, I just walked right down. When I arrived Lynn began asking me questions.

"Is there any redness there?"

"No." I replied.

"Feel the walls, what do they feel like?"

"Hard, tough. There is a little elastic give. It's like a room and there is a boulder in the middle."

"What does the boulder feel like?"

"It's hard and smooth on the outside, but it crumbles easily. I could pull it apart if I wanted to."

"What symbol is connected with the boulder?"

After examining the boulder again, I replied, "A cross."

"Ask your warrioress the meaning of this boulder with a cross on it."

Quickly vizualizing my warrioress, I did as Lynn commanded, then replied, "She says it is intellectualized spirituality."

"Ask your warrior," said Lynn.

"He says I need to express myself."

Then Lynn told me to bring the boulder up out of my throat and throw it far out into the atmosphere where it would burn up, become a bright light and disappear. I did so. My throat problems disappeared even before I made a throat bundle, as she instructed, containing symbols of this experience.

Much of what Lynn learned from her medicine teachers requires the letting go of mental mind and instead living in body mind and dream body. Making shields, masks, fetishes, bundles, songs, ceremony--all these acts objectify spiritual and psychological knowledge not only so that it can be seen and understood by the observing ego, but also learned, memorized through all the cells of the body. Rather than intellectualized knowledge, it is knowledge acquired through direct, literally hands-on experience.

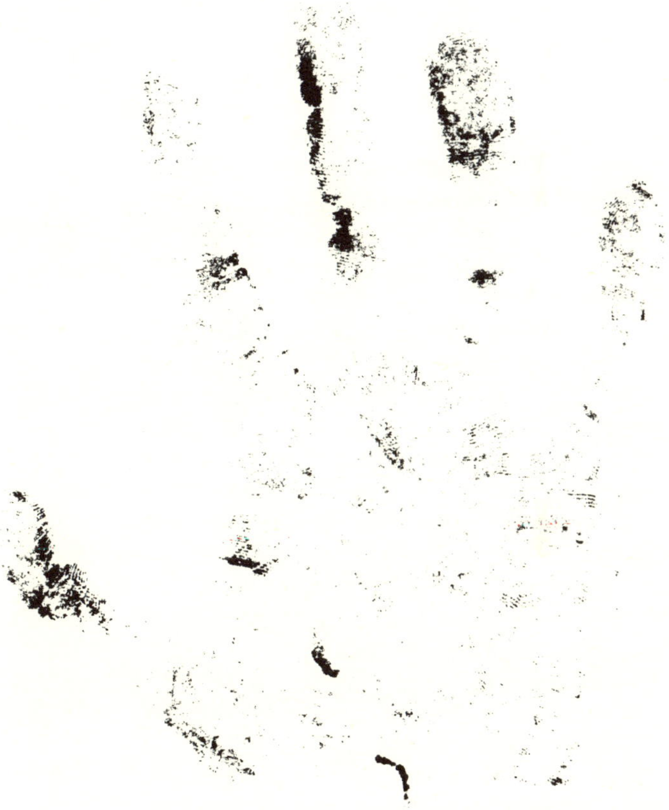

THE MOTHERS

Women and men alike must learn to understand the spirits and powers (sometimes called archetypes) that influence them. One way we women can acquire such knowledge is by making masks of the mother archetypes described in *Jaguar Woman.*

Each woman will identify one of two Final Mothers (la ultime Madre) as the one manifesting most distinctly in herself. She will be either a nurturing Great Mother, associated with birthgiving, caregiving, hearth, ovens, harvest and taking care of business; or she will be a Rainbow Mother, "the energy of the poet, dancer, weaver, seer."[9] She is the shining mother, the inspiring muse, the youthful energy behind all creative endeavor.

However, each of these Mothers has a contrary or opposite pole. On the life arrow, opposite the nurturing Great Mother is the devouring Death Mother--she who takes away life. On the level of daily human experience, a nurturing mother can become devouring when she carries her nurturing too far, assimilating her children to herself, unable to acknowledge their separateness, their unique selfhood. On the spiritual arrow, opposite the Rainbow Mother, is the Teeth Mother, also known as Crazy Woman or Medusa. When she is present, the creative flow and play congeals. She does not kill; she just maims or turns one to stone.

These four Mothers are four directions of one circle. Men also contain and attract the energies of these Mother archetypes and often relate to women as they relate to the Mothers. It is important to make a mask or fetish of the negative Mothers as well as of the positive Mothers, because *it is the negative Mothers that we choose not to look at that rule our lives.* These Mothers must be acknowledged--I feel you, I know you, I know you are there.

Although you can read about the four Mothers in *Jaguar Woman* and find them acknowledged under various names in modern psychology, to know them and to recognize how they manifest in your life, it helps to experience them--through your hands in the making of a fetish, through your body as you dance a mask, through the people who mirror them in your daily experience, as in the following narrative.

TWO STONES

I hold the bow and lance of authority!
I hold the fire and the herbal sweet grass of authority!
I hold my own authority!

from *Song of Heyoehkah*
by Hyemeyohsts Storm

I walked into the restaurant carrying a long-stemmed pink rose. It felt good to be giving it. I had made my decision to leave the teacher waiting for me at one of the tables here and to return to my home town; but I was leaving without bitterness, or at least trying to rise above it with this offering.

When I had arrived at the "camp" three months before, after finding a home nearby for myself and my mare and her foal, the man whose medicine apprentice I wanted to become had assigned me to her. She was to be my teacher. I knew her from previous visits and perceived her as a sister, a fellow apprentice rather than a teacher, one who had acquired a little knowledge here, but no wisdom, not yet. She was the Keeper of the medicine wheel on her property and had created a beautiful flower garden, also a medicine wheel; but she wanted me to agree with her, even when I disagreed. Although she seemed to expect it of me, I would not give away my own authority to her. She and others in the camp thought me disrespectful as a result.

"Get rid of the horses," she would say. "They are holding you back."

"No, I will not give up the horses. Through them I take care of the girl child in myself. They are a heart path."

"Heart is in the North," she would say, "because four is in the North and heart is a four, the fourth chackra. Mind also is a four and in the North. Therefore heart and mind are the same thing."

"No they aren't," I would reply. "A wise person within me told me once that heart teaches mind, and mind walks heart into the world in song, dance, writing, painting and many other ways. Anyway heart is in the South. I don't want to learn things the wrong way. Your own teacher teaches that heart is in the South."

She would sneer and redden and be angry with me for disagreeing with her. We went round and round with this petty, dogmatic arguing that has nothing to do with real knowledge; but I was told by others in the camp that if I could not learn from her, no one would teach me. I had learned from Lynn that the first rule of a warrioress is *respect* on the medicine path, respect for the spirit within each of us--even if you don't like a person. An apprentice must learn the art and act of respect. So I tried to accept this woman, who did indeed have many admirable qualities when she wasn't playing tough-ass medicine woman.

"Think. You must think!" she would say and try to make me define every word I used, never to her satisfaction. Archetype--she hated the word "archetype."

"It means things like Kachinas," I tried to explain, "and the Goddess, and warrioress and wise old woman. They are patterns of being. If you have a better word, I will use it, but it is the only one I know."

She made me feel so dumb, backing me into thought corners until I would clam up in resentment. "Think, think," she would pressure.

Finally, to fend off her badgering, I said, "I don't like to think!" Oh, that made her snarl.

I visited another woman in the camp, younger than myself. Greeting me at the door with her white shepherd dog at her side, she invited me in for a cup of tea.

"You are the Goddess," she said.

Although I understood the intent of her words, I chose to be contrary. "No, I'm not," I answered. I am a limited human being. She is an archetype. She manifests herself in all women and in all that is female in the world. She is the Earth. How can I say that I am the Goddess?"

"You are a tough nut to crack," she muttered.

Then she commanded me to get into my car and drive around using precious gas while she said, pointing to a school, "That is your authority!" and to the fire station, "That is your authority!" and to the police station, "That is your authority!" and to the post office, "That is your authority!" and so on in an authoritarian voice.

I just watched the road, jaws clenched, wondering, "Who do you think you are? What a nut!" Although I knew she was imitating her own teacher, I raged inside, wondering how long I could contain the volcano.

At her home once again, she showed me her garden of herbs planted to form a medicine wheel, each direction containing different plants. It was beautiful, a circle of green spirit. She was learning from the plants themselves how they were to be used. For that I respected her. Still the martinet, into the center of the herb circle she marched me.

"Sit there!" she commanded.

I sat, fuming. In front of me she placed a mirror.

"Look, there," she ordered, still adamant. "There is your authority. Sit there and meditate for awhile."

"If you are my authority, " I said to myself in the mirror, "I am damn well going to own you and show this lady what that means!" It frightened me a bit, in spite of my intent, to move against this woman's intimidating, commanding strength; but I stood up, knowing that my action took her by surprise, and walked out of the circle.

She was sitting at a picnic table, just outside the garden. I walked over, muscles tight, fight-ready, and sat down opposite her.

"Well! That's the first time anyone stayed there for only half a minute," she commented acidly.

I remained silent, looking at the weathered grain of the gray table through my dark glasses.

She remained silent.

Finally, when the silence had become softer, I said softly, "I am angry. You have been power-tripping. It makes me angry."

"That is not what I was doing," she protested, "not how it was meant."

"That is how it felt to me," I replied. "It is just so."

After another period of silence, I said, "I came to ask you how you experience the teaching here. How have you changed in the eight months you have been here?"

Then she began talking about herself, her feelings, her pain, her confusion and her seeking for the last fifteen years. Taking my dark glasses off so she could see my eyes, I looked at her with appreciation, respect, and love. She spoke to me now from the heart.

When she finished, we were quiet again until I said, "I think I will go now. There is no more to be said."

She nodded her agreement.

We shook hands with contained warmth, sincerity, for we had met one another; then I drove away, slowly, up the rutted dirt driveway.

When my appointed teacher heard about my meeting with the other woman, she criticized me for expressing my anger.

"I expressed my anger," I explained,"but I was not identified with it. I did not attack or rage. I respect my feelings."

"Anger is stupid." she said.

"I disagree" I replied.

The sneer came to her face. I had angered her once again.

Now, in the restaurant, I presented her with the rose.

"Here," I said, "in thanks for your time and your teaching over the past three months. I am glad I could see you this one last time, since it has not always been good between us. I want you to know that I recognize and appreciate your dedication to the Earth Mother Wheel and to the Goddess."

She did not accept the rose. I laid it down on the table between us as, instead, she began to talk about dogs running loose, biting children, killing fawns, running down the deer, how people should be responsible for their dogs and lock them up. Then reaching into her big purse, she pulled out a can of dog food and placed it on the table on my side of the rose.

"This is a gift for you," she said, "for you are a wild dog."

I had seen her stalking me when she first began to talk about the dogs. My shield was already up. There was a light that felt protective up to my right in the corner of my vision. Otherwise, I would never have thought to raise the shield. I had never done so before when attacked by other members of this camp and usually ended up sobbing uncontrollably for hours.

It was a large, round mirror shield, so that everything she was about to say would reflect back at her. Holding the shield in front of my stomach and heart as she spoke to me in a cold, hard voice, I held her gaze, eye to eye, equally cold, hard, steady, unflinching, Medusa reflecting Medusa, two stones.

She described a burning barn, horses and a little girl screaming inside. She described my rescuing the horses and leaving the little girl screaming, burning.

With difficulty, I maintained my polite and silent exterior while I thought such things to myself as "You're crazy, woman! You're full of shit as a Christmas turkey!"

When she finally finished her tirade after saying many more obnoxious and hurtful things, she picked up the rose and acknowledged the gift. Commanding me to remain there and meditate on her words, she said she would be back in a few minutes after paying her bill. When she stood up, however, I too rose and shook her hand very politely, nodded curtly, saying nothing, stone face.

After she walked away, I left the restaurant, leaving the rose and the dog food lying upon the table.

Teeth Mother fetish
made from a rock and shells

SPIRIT MASK JOURNEY

When Lynn Andrews first asked her small group of apprentices to make masks, I chose to make a horse mask resembling my mare. To make the mask "stand up", that is, to imbue it with power, she told us to sing the song of the spirit of the mask as we fashioned it.

My first attempt to make a mask in the company of the group was a disaster. I became angry and frustrated at my lack of artistic ability. I just could not figure out how to sculpture the head of a horse with bailing wire, tin foil and plaster cast.

In the privacy of my back yard I tried once again, running often to the corral to see how a horse's head *really* looks. It was a revelation to run my eyes and fingers over my mare's face, noticing for the first time the underlying structure of her skull, the set of her eyes, the breadth of her nose, curves, angles, connections. Full of the wonder of her, I found her song and sang it as I shaped the mask.

With another member of the group from Santa Barbara, I drove down to Lynn's house in Beverly Hills. My companion had made a medusa mask that was so powerfully ugly that when I first saw it, I felt as if I had been punched in my solar plexus. To me it looked like a spider head, black and hairy with yarn and snakey braids. The two masks, mare and medusa, rode side by side in the back of the station wagon, each wrapped in shawls. Perhaps it was their proximity that influenced later events.

In Lynn's living room we lay in a circle, our feet towards the center pole, a 4 x 4 beam entwined with red chili pepper light bulbs. High on the pole hung a cow skull. Aside from the chili peppers, only candle light and firelight from the hearth illuminated the room with a soft yellow glow. Our masks lay across our stomachs. We were about to descend through a *sipapu*, a hole in the earth, into the underworld to find the spirits of our masks.

Stamping her foot on the floor several times, Lynn called loudly, commanding the spirits to wake up. Then she began beating the drum.

Closing my eyes, I looked for a hole through which to descend. After narrowing the possibilities down to two, I stopped to wonder whether to jump in feet first or head first. It occurred to me that Alice's rabbit medicine might be helpful at a time like this. Finally, pushed by the drum beat (and worried that the drumming would end even before I began my journey) I plunged into the hole where I had buried the afterbirth of Isharra's foal. I came out of the downward tunnel between two rows of huge stone figures, closely packed like a wall on either side of me. They seemed royal and benevolent and mostly male.

As I walked forward down the row, I came to a stone figure or door that looked like a big black spider abdomen. Jungle lay all around and behind it. I knew I shouldn't go through that door; yet I needed to find the horse spirit. Finally I just stood there and whistled the same signal by which I have always called my horses in from pasture. And she burst through the foliage to the left of the spider door--a beautiful sorrel mare. As we greeted each other with affectionate gestures, I felt relieved and reassured.

Then I mounted her; and, in a stately parade gait, we proceeded up a canyon. People lining both sides of the canyon were cheering as we ascended toward a mesa with one lone tree. When we arrived at the top, I turned my spirit horse with a flourish to face the crowd. Horrified, I realized that my face was covered by the ugly black medusa mask; I could not get it off. Frightened and anxious, verging on panic, I fled on my horse to the bottom of the canyon and ascended once more. Still I could not rid myself of that mask. I fled to the bottom and ascended two more times.

For the fourth ascent I dismounted at the bottom and humbly walked beside my horse up the steep grade. After the arduous climb to the top, I groomed her lovingly, paying special attention to massaging her legs. The medusa mask disappeared. I had my own face again. I had to get off my high horse, give up my inflation, find the right relation to the horse spirit and to the surrounding people, before I could become myself.

The drums became silent. Exhausted, I returned thankfully to the warm glow of Lynn's living room. We all sat up then with our masks on. Lynn came round to each of us, tapped us each hard on the head with her knuckles and blew as though to blow the mask spirits into the crowns of our heads, followed by a shower of corn meal. As the corn meal fell around me, it felt like a gossamer net of blessing.

Then we each danced our masks, one at a time, to the beat of the drums, knowing with our bodies the nature of the spirit we had called.

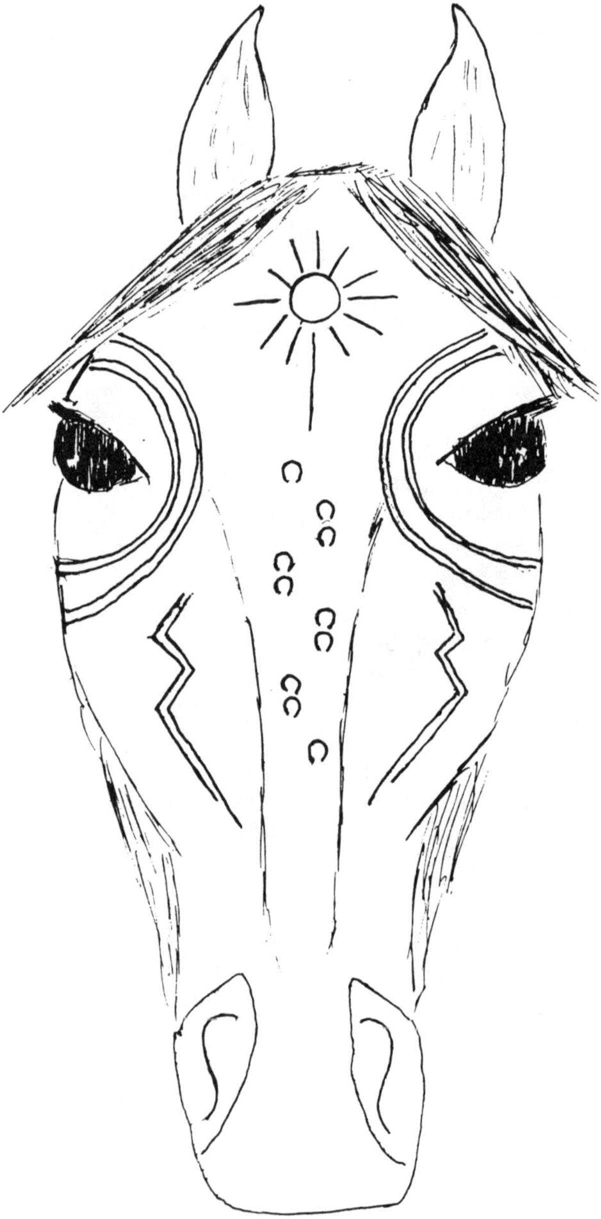

HOW TO MAKE A MASK

One traditional way to make a mask is to sculpt it out of wood. If you have the skill for that, go ahead. If you don't, here are some alternatives. Whichever method you choose, sing a song for the mask in syllables or words as you work. Some syllables from which you might choose are A, NA, MA, KA, TA, NE, HE, TAY. Some of these sounds will feel good; others will not.

Wire based mask. This type of mask is made of coat hangers or bailing wire, plaster cast, tin foil, sculptamold or similar product, plaster of paris, jesso, acrylic paint. Every mask will be different, so I'll only give you a few pointers to get you started. Use your own ingenuity to carry on.

1. Shape the underlying structure or skeleton of your mask with coat hanger wire or bailing wire. Bailing wire is the more pliable of the two and can be acquired at the nearest stable. Pliers and/or wire cutters will help you twist and cut the wire as needed. If you don't have wire cutters, go ahead and ruin a pair of scissors. At this point in the process you must decide whether you are making a simple frontal mask or a scullcap mask. The latter will fit over the crown of your head like a cap as well as over your face. Fit it loosely to your head and face size; otherwise it will be too tight after you have added layers of plaster cast. Not all masks are flat. Animal masks, especially, have three dimensional faces. Think what a long beak a hummingbird has.

2. Cover the wire skeleton with tin foil. It wraps easily over and around the wire. Newspaper(wet or dry) stuffed inside the skeleton will give some substance against which to press.

3. Cover the wire and tin foil structure with plaster cast, which may be bought at hobby, art, or hospital supply stores. Cut strips of plaster cast as needed. You will have to determine correct lengths yourself. After dipping each strip in water, lay it over the mask, wrapping the ends under the wire at each side of the mask. Layer each new strip over the edges of the last. These strips will harden into position. Leaving holes for the eyes and mouth is optional; but DO leave some opening through which to breath, usually at the nose of your mask. If you do not leave eye holes, be sure you can see out somewhere, such as below the mask or through the nose holes.

4. After the plaster cast has dried, cover the mask with a smooth layer of either plaster of paris or gesso, a base for acrylics. Plaster of paris is sturdier; gesso is lighter weight. If you choose gesso, your mask will be stronger with a least two layers of plaster cast underneath. (I have heard of using spackle at this stage, but I have not yet tried it.)

5. For ridges, ears, eyes, noses and other detailing, shape with sculptamold. Larger ears, such as horse ears, will have to be wired along with the rest of the mask. Small ears, such as skunk ears, can be sculptamolded.

6. Paint the mask with acrylic paint.

* * * *

Face based mask. Your own face is the structure for this type of mask. It is helpful to have a friend handy to lay the plaster cast over your face while you remain lying on your back.

1. Grease your face with vaseline after tying your hair well out of the way. Be sure to protect your eyebrows, hairline, and mustache thoroughly with the vaseline or you're likely to lose them painfully when you lift the mask off later.

2. Have your friend lay wet strips of plaster cast over your face. **DO NOT** cover eyes, nostrils or mouth. Apply at least two layers, folding ends neatly at the edges of the mask. Let dry in place, then lift it off your face.

3. Cover the mask with a smooth layer of either plaster of paris or jesso.

4. For detailing, shape with sculptamold or similar product.

5. Paint the mask with acrylic paint. Attach yarn, hair, feathers, ribbons--whatever you need to complete the mask.

* * * *

Paper plate mask. Draw a mask on a paper plate with color crayons or paint.

* * * *

NOTE: Inside of each mask that your make, paint a symbol of its opposite. For example, inside of a teeth mother/medusa mask, you might paint a rainbow for rainbow mother. To recoin an old cliche--they are two sides of the same mask.

* * * *

Now that you have a mask and a song, it is time to dance the mask. The mask can be danced without the underworld journey to retrieve the spirit of the mask, but also without the same degree of insight. This is one exercise that is best done in company, preferably of an experienced guide who knows you well, who will limit the duration of the dance with her drumbeat and offer support as needed. It is not desirable that you become completely possessed by the spirit of the mask; *conscious* experience is the goal. If you are not ready yet to dance, that is o.k. You will have learned much from making the mask. In these matters it is best to operate on Indian time.

CHAPTER FIVE

FEMALE AND MALE BALANCE

WARRIORESS AND WARRIOR

Lynn Andrews learned from her teachers that medicine is harmony. Female and male energy is a continuous interplay of movement within one indivisible whole. A warrioress is flexible, moving with either force without losing central rootedness in the sacred.

In her first book, *Medicine Woman,* Lynn had to develop and strengthen the feminine within herself first by developing as a huntress and warrioress, then by stealing the marriage basket from the sorcerer Red Dog. The marriage basket is a symbol of the wombness of women, the knowledge that all things are born of women, or the "feminine principle", both in nature and in the mind. The marriage basket also symbolizes the accomplishment of feminine and masculine balance, a marriage of the two. Lynn had to steal the marriage basket without being overwhelmed by masculine, patriarchal power, represented by Red Dog. Every woman must accomplish this task in her own way.

It is extremely important for women to reflect the Feminine into ceremony. All too often women have learned from male teachers. Imitating men both in ceremony and in daily life, they fail in their task to reflect the feminine half of the balance into the proceedings. A woman must remember who she is. She must develop a spirit place in dream work and ceremony and realize the power of her original nature so that she cannot be disconcerted, disturbed or agitated off her true center. Lynn Andrew's teachers taught her that women carry the void from which all things are born; women's source is the vortex of whirlpool or wind.

Understanding the meaning of concepts such as "the Feminine" or "the Void" is not accomplished through dictionary definition or categorization. This understanding will unfold in a feminine way like a rose, petal by petal, into full bloom through your experience of life and through the mirroring of a few books and teachers.

To aid the understanding of feminine and masculine balance, even without the guidance of a medicine woman you can vizualize the warrioress and warrior within yourself and talk with each of them or write them letters. Both warrioress and warrior are guardians, connections, messengers between the conscious and subconscious mind, between tonal and nagual, or, in other words, between the ego and the Self. A woman may search all her life for the perfect male, but all outer relationships will be incomplete until she has found her inner male. Likewise, a man must connect to his inner female.

In *Jaguar Woman*, the medicine woman Zoila calls these inner beings the "sacred twins" and explains that they are called warrior and warrioress because they "fight for the balance of your consciousness."[10]

When I first visualized and spoke to my warrioress, her wisdom brought great relief to me. She had long blond hair, beauty and strength of body. She carried a shield and a lance. I was possessed by a great anger at that time in my life, murderous anger at a man and anger at myself for giving away my power, falling into his manipulative traps. I felt he had taken something from me, besides my self-esteem, at a deep, subtle level; for he was one who knew something of sorcery. I was full of hate and in bad shape.

This beautiful guardian warrioress said to me: "Go with the wind, Jan. Become strong together with your mare. Find the song of her again. Fly with it. The life energy flows always within the earth mother. What is lost can be regained. What has been given away or taken away--let it go. Give it to the universe and to the human family. It never was yours to own. Recognize the treasure for what it is. You are its vessel and must become a worthy container."

Her words began my healing.

Another time, after I had asked her if she liked being with me in my life, she replied: "Yes, Jan, I do. But you have become timid. Your steps are awkward and slow in the dance of love and life. Enter the whirlwind. Dance to the stars and back to earth again. Run laughing into the world, yet touch your world gently. Let every gesture be a dance of love and life, love *for* life. Feel the dance with me now, swaying your body. Move always from the quiet, centered core, the flower....

It was more difficult for me to vizualize my warrior. The first time I tried to connect with him, I was sitting in pasture with my horses--Isharra and her new foal--writing a letter to him.

"Dear Warrior," I began. "I salute you. I take your hand."

I stopped writing then, followed my horses around for awhile in the unfenced area, and began singing a song that came to me. As I sang, an antlered deer came out of the brush, calmly passing in front of me. He had a white tail with a black tip and was slightly lame in his right foreleg. He walked across the field until he disappeared behind bushes and trees at the other side.

As he went by I called out to him. "Are you not completely well? I send my love to you. I wish you healing. Thank you for this song."

Later I spoke with this deer in my imagination, saying, "Beautiful deer, magically appearing out of the brush as I sang a song to my warrior. Why did you cross the field?"

"I sought water," he replied, "to quench the thirst of spirit and body."

"I was glad to see you." Your appearance was a gift."

"I am looking out for you. Consider the nature of my maleness. Not aggressive, but graceful, gentle, efficient in being. A spirit for leaping over obstacles, gliding through thickets as if they were only water, blending with the background except when I choose to show myself, at home in day or night, although morning and evening are my best times. My antlers are my pride, but they also make me a target. Let the deer walk proudly, even though a little wary of the enemy. There is strength, no shame, in keeping out of sight or running to safer places. I crossed your vision. My magic belongs to you."

I have since spoken to my warrior in human form, but it is for you to discover and speak to your own warrioress and warrior, as I shall next explain how to do.

HOW TO BECOME ACQUAINTED WITH YOUR WARRIOR AND WARRIORESS

1. Vizualize your inner warrioress and warrior. Note details of their appearance and dress.

2. Write each of them a letter.

3. Dialog with them. Speaking to each of them separately, ask them their names. Ask them if they like being with you. Tell them your needs and feelings. Be especially strong with your warrior if necessary. Ask them what they think of each other. Thank them for being with you. When I partake in such a conversation, I find it helpful to record the dialog in writing as it occurs.

4. Make a fetish of both your warrioress and your warrior. A fetish can be sculpted, painted, or created out of anything and everything in the environment which will express their nature.

CHAPTER SIX

STRENGTHENING YOUR TONAL

Agnes Whistling Elk taught that physical strength, connection to and love for your body is important on a spiritual path. The more you begin to develop spiritually, the more you need to keep your physical body in good shape. Spiritual energy might be compared to an electrical charge--you can't run 220 volts through a 110 volt appliance; it would burn out.

While it would be a dramatic adventure to be sent running between the cabins of two medicine women in Canada, as Lynn was, we urban women and men can accomplish the same thing through jogging, dancing, sports, martial arts, hiking, gardening, cleaning house or shoveling manure.

Keeping your body in shape is only part of keeping your *tonal* strong. *Tonal* refers particularly to the guardian spirit, totem, or medicine animal--the unique personality--with which you were born. It might be compared to the sun sign of astrology. More broadly, it refers to your physical being in the daytime world that you usually call reality.

If you went to a Native American medicine woman for teaching, she might have you chop wood for two years before teaching you anything. The point is--it is necessary to be well-grounded in the ordinary reality of working, eating, relationships and keeping a roof over your head, the reality in which we have to earn x number of dollars to qualify for a home loan.

One especially boring secretarial job became tolerable to me when I recognized it as the "woodchopping" part of my training. I remember a day on that job at which my routine tasks included answering the phone, answering the callers' questions or routing the calls to another department. During a lull in the phone traffic, I found myself on a prairie path, flat at first, then leading up a mountain. Phone calls interrupted my journey, but I kept returning to the path after taking care of the business at hand because I wanted to find out where it went. Eventually I followed it to the mouth of a cave about halfway up the mountain. Inside the cave was a crystal cavern, all blue crystals. On an altar in the center of the cavern stood a woman in blue, shining with blue light.

"Sing blue light," she said to me. "Write blue light."

I knew I must learn what she meant, then do it as my calling, my vocation. After speaking with her briefly, I retraced my steps down the trail to the starting point, answering yet another phone call on my return.

The *tonal* is the doing side of power, as compared to the *nagual*, which is the unknown, the mystery, the other reality, the realm of the blue woman. The center of the *tonal* is reason, while the center of the *nagual* is will--the purpose of your being, the path of the inner Self. We must strengthen the *tonal* so that the will becomes clear, and so that reason will not disintegrate when we confront the *nagual*. Then we can move between the two with the help of our translators, who are our warrior and warrioress.

Being strong in your *tonal* means having the power to bring your dream of life into reality, to turn spirit into substance in your life, to make an act of beauty, whether it be beading a belt, weaving a blanket, writing a book, building a house, training a horse, healing others or caring for the needy. The danger is otherwise to become lost in the ozone of intellectualized spirituality, insanity, alcoholism or other addictions, fanaticism, or helplessness and despair.

This "doing" side of power does not preclude receptivity or just "being", nor is it driven or controlled by the desire for social status and approval; rather, an act of power and beauty is in harmony with the natural cycle of creativity that includes receptivity, impregnation through illumination and experience, waiting for the seed to develop within, and finally laboring to bring it forth into the daylight--a most natural kind of childbirth. It is an act that requires the strength and perseverance, the gentleness and devotion of a mare, a creature of the earth who roams over the earth without bound.

To describe this "doing" yet another way, from the point of view of the adventurous, playful boy and sacred clown in the East of my medicine wheel: Concentrate. Watch and wait for the ideas, messages. There is time. Be in it. Use it. Time is a gift for you. Play with the demands of the outer world. You do not need to feel pushed, pressured. Play. Take risks. Try things out. Learn to play creatively in space and time. At the same time you will be responsible by bringing to birth. That is the paradox.

Strengthening your *tonal*, therefore, is part of what it means to walk in balance, caring intentionally for both your inner and outer realities. More playfully, the next time you are flossing your teeth in front of your bathroom mirror, be mindful that this act too is part of your striving toward wholeness and balance and is sacred. Then chuckle over that thought. A sense of humor, too, will keep you in balance.

CHAPTER SEVEN

POWER

Ask not for power,
ask only for understanding
-an inner teacher

Just as a kitchen knife can be used to slice carrots and tomatoes for a healthy salad or to slice someone's throat, power also can be used for either creative or destructive purposes. Because power is associated with those who manipulate and control others, it has gotten a bad name. We fear and refuse it; others seek it for that very purpose.

However, the root meaning of power (American Heritage Dictionary, 2nd ed.) is simply "to be able". Good medicine will en-able, not dis-able or enslave you. You in turn must take the responsibility for your ableness or ability.

Healers, teachers and people in many other walks of life who have expanded their capabilities do sometimes use their power, their ableness, to dominate others or to bask in the adulation of followers. It would be naive not to acknowledge that. Also, with quite good intentions, a person of power may take away or bypass another's self-authority, thus creating more bondage.

For example, I once went to a lecture where a healer who used sound, which she said she channeled from her spirit guide, uttered a few notes in demonstration during her talk. The intent of the notes, she explained to the audience, was to produce clarity. This "laser" sound, which (I later learned) affects subtle energy centers of the body called *chackras*, had a powerful effect on me as well as on other members of the audience. One woman felt her "stomach" spinning like a whirligig. For a few moments I could not gather my will to get up from my seat. There was no ill intention behind her demonstration. She was displaying her wares, so to speak, to drum up business. But I had not given her permission to do this to me. I did not know, at the time, that sound could be used in such a way, so I had no way to protect myself from the intrusion. As for acquiring clarity--I would prefer to do so by my own efforts, thank you anyway.

Seekers for knowledge often mistake a teacher's power for spirituality. It's impressive when a person of power can call a thousand frogs out of a river to croak at your feet, produce a thunderstorm where none was brewing, or channel healing light through a crystal. While power and spirituality are sometimes closely connected, they must not be confused with one another. The ultimate goal on the medicine path is not power, but enlightenment. In *Star Woman* a medicine woman explains that we come to this earthwalk for only one reason--to become one with the Great Spirit, like an ice cube melting into the ocean. "You come to a teacher...and that teacher holds up a mirror. And if you're willing to look into it, the mirror becomes like the sun and you begin to heat up. You begin to melt into that ocean."[11]

In *Flight of the Seventh Moon,* Agnes Whistling Elk describes in an effective and beautiful way the correct understanding of medicine power:

> Power, in my way, is the *understanding* of the spirit of medicine energy that flows through all beings. A medicine person can translate that energy into healing and transformation for herself and others. Power is the strength and ability to see yourself through your own eyes and not through the eyes of another. It is being able to place a circle of power at your own feet and not take power from someone else's circle. True power is love.[12]

CHAPTER EIGHT

THE SACRED SPIRAL

Addictions come in many guises. Most of us recognize the most obvious kinds--addiction to alcohol, nicotine, drugs, coffee, sugar. Following is a list of addictions that often go unrecognized. Once you get the idea, you can make a list that applies specifically to you, i.e., **WITNESS YOUR ADDICTIONS!**

To name just a few, there are addictions to

Fear	Sex
Fear of success	Power
Fear of failure	Being a victim
Poverty	Excuses
Hoarding	"I can't"
Spending	"There are no jobs"
Perfection	"No one recognizes my ability"
Approval of others	Winning
Wealth	Control
A man (woman)	Dramatic moments
Men who aren't right for you	Children
Pets	etc.

Addictions make you feel safe but prevent you from reclaiming your original nature.

Among Native American peoples, a symbol is frequently found that expresses and teaches of the process by which each human being journeys through life away from her or his center, accumulating addictions on the way. This symbol is the spiral; it is also a map of the way back to the center, to enlightenment. One of my inner teachers likes to call that center place "the loving heart of ages forever."

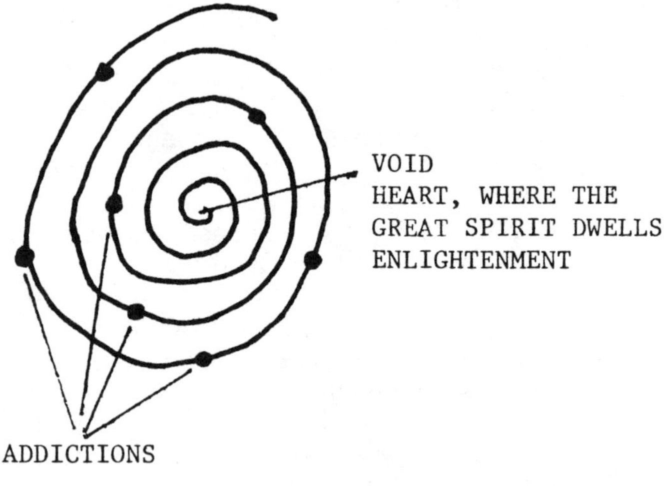

THE SACRED SPIRAL

Lynn Andrews vividly describes this spiral and attendant addictions in *Jaguar Woman* in the chapter "La Caldera and the Sacred Spiral". At the bottom of La Caldera, the deep pit of an old volcano accessible by a spiraling path, was a whirlpool--yet another mirror of the spiral. Lynn told me once that a woman goes into the whirlpool when she goes into her power. More than once, she told me to go to a stream and meditate upon the whirlpool eddies there. When it came time to go down to find the spirit of the skunk mask I had made, it was into a pool of water that I dove, a pool of that same stream, surrounded by huge sandstone boulders, sycamore trees, and chaparral. The starting point was again Lynn's living room, a circle of women around the center pole, the drum beating in background and brain.

Into the whirling, churning water I dove at the base of a waterfall. I surfaced in a round, quiet pond surrounded by lush tropical trees and flowers. Leaving the pond, I began to forge among the trees, calling the skunk. Then a voice told me to remain at the pond, to see and feel the beauty around me. I did so, first noticing the color, beauty and profusion of the large, lush blooms, the stillness of the pond, and the rich green framing it all. Then I closed my eyes to feel the peace, gentleness, and joy of the place.

When I opened my eyes, I noticed a strange being on a rock in the center of the pond. Entering the water once again, I swam over to examine it. It looked like a large square golden mask, but alive. Behind it the skunk was hiding. The two seemed to be connected, although not physically. I laughed happily when I discovered him there. Taking him in my arms, I dove deep into the pond and resurfaced in the pool among the boulders. Climbing out, I lay naked in the sun on the warm rocks, the skunk lying beside me. Then he climbed onto my stomach and began kneading my abdomen like a cat. Minor pains that I had been chronically experiencing in my abdomen disappeared thereafter. Finally he lay on my stomach (where the skunk mask actually rested).

Suddenly the square golden mask appeared upright on the rocks in front of me, transformed into a single eye, then into an eagle that soared above us into the sky over the canyon.

As I danced the skunk mask afterward, I discovered the spirit to be full of play and curiosity, sticking his nose into everything, a clown who delighted in arousing laughter and, through his antics, calming the fear of the woman who was about to dance a Death Mother mask.

* * * * * * * * * * * * * *

Wherever a spiral is painted, such as on a cave wall, another picture very often accompanies it. It is an image of the humpbacked flute player, who brings the fructifying rain wherever he goes. He is one who cares lovingly but who takes in and gives away unselfishly. He does not grasp and hold or attach himself to things; he touches the earth lightly.

A similar image is the Rainmaker of an old Chinese story. When he was called to an arid place to make rain, he just went about his ordinary business in the solitary dwelling that was loaned to him, and on the third day the rain came. Rainmakers are very inconspicuous, wrote Irene Claremont de Castillejo in *Knowing Woman.* Yet life blossoms all around them without their seeming to lift a finger.

> The Rainmaker does not cause, he *allows* the rain to fall...In those rare moments when all the opposites meet within a man, good and also evil, light and also darkness, spirit and also body, brain and also heart, masculine focused consciousness and at the same time feminine diffuse awareness, wisdom of maturity and childlike wonder; when all are allowed and none displaces any other in the mind of a man, then that man, though he may utter no word, is in an attitude of prayer. Whether he knows it or not, his own receptive allowing will affect all those around him; rain will fall on the parched fields, and tears will turn bitter grief to flowering sorrow, while stricken children dry their eyes and laugh.[13]

This is also the way of the warrioress, who "faces the world lightly, like a plume" rather than remaining "rooted in a swamp of addictions."[14]

I remember one evening during which I sat alone in my room wallowing in several of my addictions. I had a headache, my friends never called, I was a failure, I was no good, I felt lousy, etc. Then I recalled a man who had introduced himself to me in a dream a year before. He had said then that he was from a place called Unteroben and had fought in the underground during the War (an aspect of my inner warrior, although I did not know of such things at the time.) I had spoken to him then and found him to be a kindly guide. Wondering if he could help me now, I called him into my mind.

Man from Unteroben, I feel the need of light. Can you give it to me?

Find it yourself in your heart.

What do you mean?

Loving heart of ages forever, as the Old Woman said.

How do I get there? How shall I feel it?

Give to someone.

What about loving a man? I'm so confused about that.

There are inner and outer men. Both need your love. You are on the right track. Stay close to the heart. That's where the meaning is.

It's so hard to translate your messages sometimes into outer behavior.

Take it slowly. One step at a time.
Love your keeper. You've heard that before.

I don't know my keeper.

You know him. He is everyone.

Yes, the one in all.

My hand is on your head. The headache will go.
Feel warmth, love and warmth, like a cocoon.
Let it surround you. Let the ring surround you.

Sun light, light of the sun
Sun light, O my darling,
Live on a blue cloud
Live on the earth

Go into the heart of things
Glory and wholeness
Wonder in love
Love in exaltation
Give of your heart
Give of your soul
You will be whole
Melt ice, ice of hate and fear
Do not ask for power, only understanding
Let flow the water well into the night
Love the night
Love the day
Yours is the way
Into the heart.

I'll go now. This is enough. I feel warmer, have more strength now. Thank you for telling me the way to the sun. I'll take a step along this way. If I lose sight of it, I'll come again.

Go in peace.

Peace be with you too.

PRAYER ARROWS: A GIFT FROM THE HEART

May all your anger
All your sorrow
All your pain
Be transformed
Into love and healing power

These were the warm wishes, wrapped around a prayer arrow, that I once sent to a friend. As I wrapped the arrow-length stick with a *spiral* of sky blue, soft rose, green and multi-colored yarn, I sang the words of the prayer. This tangible prayer touched the heart of the receiver, who said it helped to heal him; it made a difference.

The gift of prayer may be given at any season, on any occasion, whenever it is needed. You may give it to yourself; you are worth it. According to a tradition of the Huichol Indians of Mexico, you must plant the prayer arrow in the earth in a place of power. There you must leave it, giving it away to the universe. Kayumari, the spirit of the deer, will come to carry the prayer to the Great Spirit.

To make a prayer arrow, you need only

1) A fairly straight stick, 1/4 inch to 1/2 inch in diameter, 12 to 20 inches long.

2) Two small feathers, 3 inches to 5 inches long.

3) Strips of yarn in any number of colors of your choice.

You may use a dowel stick bought in a hardware store or hobby shop, a length of bamboo, or a branch cut from a tree. Be sure to talk to the tree before cutting the branch, telling the tree why you need a piece of it and thanking it for its contribution. It is important to acknowledge your kinship with all living things in this way. Your whole attitude in the process of making this arrow will contribute to the meaning and power of your prayer. (If your stick is store-bought, sit out on your lawn or among your plants, touch the grass and thank all the green and growing things for their gifts to us, for even the air we breathe.) Prepare your arrow by cutting off the leaves and twigs and peeling away the bark. A sharp, small kitchen knife will do the job.

It is my common practice to pick up bird feathers in good condition whenever I see them on the ground. If you don't have any feathers, speak to the birds around your house about your need and keep your eyes open. You will soon have at least two feathers. Feathers and dyed chicken fluff may also be purchased in hobby shops.

After you have cut several strips of yarn in varying lengths (about 10 to 20 inches), you will be ready to make the prayer arrow.

1) First, place the feathers on each side of the thickest end of the arrow, holding them in place with your fingers while you secure them with the first strand of yarn, as described in the next step. If you find handling feathers and yarn at once too awkward, you might anchor the feathers first with clear tape.

2) To begin wrapping the yarn, drop the first inch of the yarn along the stick, then wrap the remaining length around that leader, the feather quills and the arrow. Continue winding the yarn around the arrow while you repeat the prayer you have chosen. Say it, sing it, chant it--whatever feels right. Sing it from your heart; sing it from your soul.

3) When you arrive near the end of the first strand of yarn, leave about 1/2 inch hanging down the

side of the arrow, while you hold it in place with your fingers. After choosing your next color, wind that new strand around the old tail and around its own bit of leader, beginning your loops where the last ones left off.

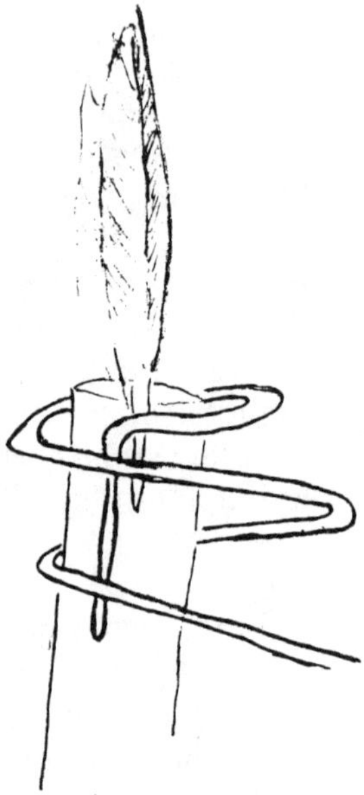

Steps 1 and 2: Securing the feathers and the yarn. Hold yarn and feathers in place with fingers while wrapping first strand around quills and its own tail end.

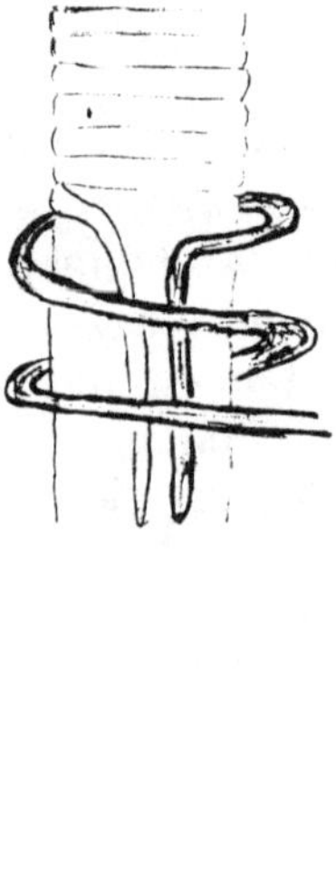

Step 3: Adding a new color of yarn. Your fingers will hold both new and old strands in place until new strand is well-started.

4) Continue down the length of the arrow, changing colors as often as you like, leaving the last two or three inches of the stick bare. The last tail of yarn can be threaded back through a loop or two above to tie it off--or just end it with a knot.

5) Tie a few colored ribbons to the arrow or suit any other creative intuition or fancy. (Dyed fluff looks pretty at the base of the two main feathers, but must be added at the beginning.) This step is optional.

6) You may plant the arrow in the earth yourself or give it as a gift. You may want to include an explanatory card for the recipient, including the prayer that you have woven into the arrow. The recipient can then do the planting.

7) To find a place of power, go out into nature and walk until you find a location in which you feel especially positive and strong. You may find such a place in your own yard, a local park or even a potted plant.

8) When you have found the right place, create a personal ceremony as you place it in the ground. For example, sing or say the prayer again toward each of the four directions and ask the spirit of the deer to take your prayer to the Great Spirit. Touch the earth with your hands, thanking the Earth Mother for all her material gifts, for dream and for imagination.

Leave the arrow where you planted it. Wind, weather or curious persons will take the arrow, but the spirit of the deer will have taken your prayer.

Step 8: Plant the arrow in the ground in a place of power.

CHAPTER NINE

CEREMONY

Just as bailing wire is used as the armature around which a mask can be structured, just as our bones are the armature for the flesh of our bodies, so ceremony is an armature for spirit. Ceremony allows spirit to have form, as may also a book, a painting, a dance, a song, and our very existence in bodily form. This book is a ceremony of trust and innocence.

Ceremony derives from a Latin word for a religious rite. *Ceremony,* as well as the name of *Ceres*, the Roman goddess of agriculture, may derive more distantly from the Indo-European root *ker*, meaning *to grow*. Often visibly dramatizing abstract psychological and spiritual concepts, ceremony is a sacrament for growth not only of grain, but also of our spirits.

Ceremonies create and give form to human movement through the cycles of the seasons, the cycles of our lives, movement from one sphere of energy to another. We cannot animate without form, which yields movement. A North ceremony, for example, will catalyze a woman's movement into the North part of the medicine wheel, where she will take responsibility for her wisdom and knowledge and give it form in her life.

A ceremony may be very simple, as when I greeted the birth of Isharra's new foal, Two Deer Moon, with a sprinkling of cornmeal, gratitude and awe; or it may be a communal, five-day affair, complex in both symbol and action.

Since ceremony is best understood by experience and example, rather than by definition, the following page describes a ceremony that you can do. It is a personal ceremony, to be enacted alone. Before you begin, purify yourself with the smoke of sage, cedar or other cleansing herb, or a bath scented with pine oil.

LIFE ARROW / DEATH ARROW CEREMONY

This ceremony takes place at the bottom and top of a mountain (such as you have within reach).

Bottom of mountain. Make a death arrow. (You may make it first at home if you prefer.) This arrow is like a prayer arrow, only it is tied with black yarn, ribbons, feathers. List on a piece of paper all the things you want to be rid of, such as pain, despair, anger, frustration, confusion, specific negative self-talk, specific addictions, etc. Place this piece of paper around the arrow shaft and wind the black yarn over it. If you use bamboo for the shaft, you can tuck the paper into the core.

Make a circle with tobacco and place the arrow in the ground at the center. Chant as you do so. Put on your Teeth Mother or Death Mother mask and dance briefly. (A paper plate/color crayon mask will do if you haven't made one of the others.) Give away the things you listed on the slip of paper. Do this OUT LOUD. Burn the arrow and bury the ashes.

Top of mountain. Make a life arrow. Tie on colors that resonate. Be sure to use some red. Put all the things you want into this arrow, such as your medicine goals, your tonal goals, what it is you are becoming. Make it beautiful.

Make a circle of tobacco and corn meal and place the arrow in the ground at the center. Name the things OUT LOUD that you put into this arrow. Wake the spirits of the place with a LOUD chant. Look around you; look at your arrow; remember the song you sang here. In the future there will be times when singing your life arrow song will revive the beauty, courage and power of this moment for you.

Leave the arrow in the ground when you go. Give it away to the universe.

CHAPTER TEN

SACRED FOOD

In a book of practical wisdom, what can be more practical than cooking and eating? Here too old wisdom can enrich our lives and show us the way.

The old hunting and gathering societies were more aware of their connection to the animals and plants upon which they depended for food than are we supermarket shoppers. Lynn Andrew's initiation with Ruby Plenty Chiefs when she arrived fresh and eager from Beverly Hills included cutting up a fresh deer carcass. Hunters in the old way said prayers over killed game, acknowledged their relationship, and thanked the animal for its give-away. Plants were also gathered with respect and thanks. Agricultural societies such as the Hopi still plant seeds and gather the harvest in ceremony, in a sacred way.

Most of us are familiar with a way of blessing food by saying grace at the dinner table. If you have forgotten this custom, adopt it once again with consciousness and intent. Thank the Great Spirit by whatever name you prefer, and thank the animals and plants, too, for their give-away. Acknowledge your place in the great web of life. (Depending on the company you are in, however, you may want to do this silently. Not everyone will understand your thanking the hypothetical pigs, cows, chickens, corn and peas that supplied the food on your plate. One Thanksgiving, during a family gathering, I thanked the turkey for its give-away. Making the connection for the first time between the meat on her dish and the fanciful birds she had been drawing in school, my six-year-old niece refused to eat a single bite.)

One woman I know spent years participating in ceremonies of various tribes. Corn, especially blue corn, was always part of the ceremony. She had the honor of preparing a ceremonial corn pudding:

> I tried to memorize every step of the preparation--proportions, cooking times, heat of the burners, everything. Nothing worked. It took two years for me to understand something...to understand, not with my mind as an idea or concept and not as a feeling, but to know with all my being: *food is sacred.* Food carries our thoughts and feelings, our prayers and Life Energy to those who eat it. The way we think or feel when we cook is more important than any recipe we could follow.[15]

With a friend of mine I once planted blue corn seeds in a circular garden on her land. We planted the seeds with prayer, song and laughter. When it was time to harvest the corn, we did so together in the same way. Then we sat on the floor of her home and scraped the kernels off ear after ear of corn. Next we ground the corn in a little hand-turned mill. It was hard work and a beautiful sharing. Some of the flour we placed in bundles to be used later in ceremony and to give as gifts. The rest we set aside for baking corn muffins for our next medicine wheel gathering.

Later I sat before my altar meditating on the ear of blue corn I had placed there. Picking up pen and paper, I wrote two words--blue corn. Then more words, unexpected words followed. With these spirit words, this spirit food, I leave you, as one medicine teacher once voiced it, "within the mirror of creativity and touching the world circle."

* * * * * * * * * * * * * *

Blue corn. Spider Woman created it. Corn meal falls around my head like a spiderweb, blessing of the shamaness. Silver strands connect us, belly to belly. You vibrate on your end; no matter the distance, it touches me. I do not need to know who you are. In the web, we are one.

One is the sun. In this oneness is illumination, consciousness, and finally, enlightenment. Sunlight glitters on the web, rainbows shimmer in the silk. In the web we are one and one is the sun. She is so dark, so terrible, yet from her weavings--light, rainbow of above and below, mirror of the universe, a medicine wheel to catch flying spirits, connecting the lonely ones within her great zero, her silver circle.

Blue corn, blue corn, food of the ancient ones, body food, spirit food, bodyspirit one. Blue corn, transforming sun into green life, blue life. Spirit of the plants, White Goddess, White Buffalo Woman, teacher of green wisdom, trust and innocence of laughing, joyous corn maidens. The corn meal falls around me. I am become a corn maiden in the lap of White Buffalo Woman.

NOTES

1. *The I Ching or Book of Changes*, tr. by Richard Wilhelm, 3rd ed. (Princeton: Princeton University Press, 1950) p.

2. June Singer, *Boundaries of the Soul* (Garden City: Anchor Press, 1972) P. 300.

3. Lynn Andrews, *Flight of the Seventh Moon: the Teaching of the Shields* (San Francisco: Harper & Row, 1984) pp. 194-195.

4. *Maria Sabina: Her Life and Chants* as told to Alvaro Estrada (Santa Barbara: Ross Erikson,) p. 94.

5. *Ibid.*, p. 105.

6. Swami Muktananda, *Kundalini: the Secret of Life* (South Fallsburg, NY: SYDA Foundation, 1979) pp. 13-14.

7. Lynn Andrews, *Jaguar Woman*(San Francisco: Harper & Row, 1985) pp. 132-133.

8. Edward Edinger, *Ego and Archetype* (Baltimore: Penguin Books, 1972) P. 100.

9. Lynn Andrews, *Jaguar Woman*, p. 47.

10. *Ibid.*, p. 134.

11. Lynn Andrews, *Star Woman* (New York: Warner Books, 1986) p. 69.

12. Lynn Andrews, *Flight of the Seventh Moon*, p. 130.

13. Irene Claremont de Castillejo, *Knowing Woman: a Feminine Psychology* (New York: Harper & Row, 1973) pp. 132-133.

14. Lynn Andrews, *Star Woman*, p. 69.

15. Celine-Marie Pascale, "Blue Corn", unpublished essay, 1985.